Oxford basics
for children
Starting and Ending Lessons

Oxford Basics series

Introduction to Teaching English

Presenting New Language

Simple Listening Activities

Simple Writing Activities

Simple Reading Activities

Simple Speaking Activities

Classroom English

Intercultural Activities

Teaching Grammar

Cross-curricular Activities

Activities Using Resources

Oxford Basics for Children series

Vocabulary Activities

Storytelling

Listen and Do

English Through Music

See the Oxford University Press ELT website at
http://www.oup.com/elt for further details.

Oxford basics
for children

Starting and Ending Lessons

NAOMI MOIR

OXFORD

UNIVERSITY PRESS

OXFORD
UNIVERSITY PRESS

Great Clarendon Street, Oxford OX2 6DP

Oxford University Press is a department of the University of Oxford.
It furthers the University's objective of excellence in research, scholarship,
and education by publishing worldwide in

Oxford New York

Auckland Cape Town Dar es Salaam Hong Kong Karachi
Kuala Lumpur Madrid Melbourne Mexico City Nairobi
New Delhi Shanghai Taipei Toronto

With offices in

Argentina Austria Brazil Chile Czech Republic France Greece
Guatemala Hungary Italy Japan Poland Portugal Singapore
South Korea Switzerland Thailand Turkey Ukraine Vietnam

OXFORD and OXFORD ENGLISH are registered trade marks of
Oxford University Press in the UK and in certain other countries

ISBN: 978 0 19 442299 4

Printed in China

ACKNOWLEDGEMENTS

Illustrations by: Paul Gibbs (Page 36) and the remainder by Heather
Clarke © Oxford University Press.

Contents

Introduction

Teaching young learners can be very unpredictable. Sometimes the children will come into class full of energy, and at other times it will be quite the opposite. Children's concentration will come and go – even on a good day! An activity can be loved in one lesson and then fall flat in the next, or just as easily work with one class and not another. Maybe an activity will take half the planned time, or it will be much harder than expected, or maybe it won't work at all.

All of these factors make lesson planning for young learners tricky. It can be very hard to judge exactly how much material you will need for a lesson. We also need to be willing and able to make changes as the lesson goes along in order to deal with some of the situations mentioned above.

In addition to the unpredictable nature of working with children, it is necessary to consider their need for constant revision and confidence-building activities, and to make them feel comfortable and happy in the classroom. Children can get a lot of pleasure from games and competitions, and they also need routines to feel safe and sure of their environment. The most crucial aspect to remember is the need for variety to keep children motivated and interested in the lesson.

The idea behind this book is to provide a range of short activities that require little or no preparation to deal with the situations outlined above. These activities can be used at the start of a lesson as warm-up activities to settle the children into their lesson and to switch them onto English. Alternatively, they can be used at the end of the lesson to fill an unexpected five or ten minutes when another activity has run short, or maybe it has run long, not leaving enough time to do whatever else was planned. They can be used at any time to bring variety to the classroom dynamics, while creating opportunities for lots of revision and recycling of language. Essentially the activities are ideas to have up your sleeve in the young learners' classroom to deal with those unexpected moments and to help meet the learning needs of under eleven-year-olds.

The activities selected range in age and level, including ideas for non-readers and writers. A lot of these ideas involve movement, but very few resources; mostly just paper, pens, the board, and simple pictures.

Starting and Ending Lessons

When exercising the body, it's important to warm up and cool down. If you jump right in with hard exercise and don't cool down when you have finished you might hurt yourself, and your body will feel the strain later, which can easily put you off wanting to do more exercise.

Learning is like exercise for the brain! Without a warm-up and a cool-down, the brain can easily feel the strain and this can put children off learning as it 'hurts', or feels too difficult.

A number of the activities in this book can be used to warm up and cool down the brain. They can become part of a 'warm up-cool down' routine. Outlined below are some suggestions for establishing a starting and ending routine to your lessons.

The start of the lesson:

- If logistically possible, have the children make a line outside the classroom door. They should greet you and make eye contact as they enter the room.
- Ask the children to sit in a circle on the floor and greet each other. If sitting on the floor is not an option, the children can sit at their tables, or their chairs can be moved into the centre of the room in a circle.
- Start the lesson with an activity that is familiar and relatively easy, such as a game they particularly like or the cool-down activity from the previous lesson.
- Ask a different child each lesson to write the date on the board.
- Encourage the children to be involved in moving any furniture or handing out the materials needed for the lesson.
- Establish a routine for where they should put their books, pencil cases, and bags. Children are easily distracted by 'things', so it is better if they can be somewhere out of sight until they need them.

The end of the lesson:

The last activity of the lesson (before closing the lesson) should be relatively easy and something the children can do without too much concentration and effort, as this is when their brains are the most tired.

- Don't shout out the instructions for homework as they walk out of the door. Write the homework clearly on the board, and make sure there are one or two minutes at the end of the lesson for them to copy it into their notebooks and to check they understand what they have to do.
- Make sure the room is tidy and as it should be before allowing any of them to leave the room.
- Stand by the door, and once they have packed up their things and pushed their chairs in, they can come to the door. Get them to make eye contact with you and say goodbye before letting them leave; *Goodbye, see you next time!*
- For older children, as they leave the classroom, get them to reflect on what they have learnt in the lesson. Each child has to think of one thing they have learnt in the lesson. It could be a piece of vocabulary, some factual information, or a sentence using the grammar point that was covered. Keep this relatively easy and don't put too much pressure on getting it right. The important thing is that they are thinking about the lesson and leave the room in a calm and controlled way.

How this book is organized

The activities in this book can be used for a number of purposes – to warm up a class, to fill a gap, or to cool down a class – many of the ideas can serve more than one purpose depending on when in the lesson you use them and what language you choose to work with. For ease of use, the activities have been divided into two groups: those which can be used with very young learners (aged four and above) are listed first, and those which can be used with older children (aged seven and above) are listed second. Many of the earlier activities can also be used with older children.

How the activities are organized

Each activity starts with a short introduction to help you plan. The introduction contains the following information:

Language: This states any specific language focus (structure or topic) of the activity. Many of the activities included can be used to revise a range of vocabulary or grammar structures. Activities that state 'vocabulary or grammar you wish to revise' can be used to fit around your syllabus. Several of the activities focus on 'learner-generated' language, which means that the language the children produce won't be specifically connected to a particular language point, but will simply be the language they produce while doing the activity.

Resources: This lists what materials and resources you need to bring to class for the activity. Most of the activities are low in resources, so quite often you will only need the board, board pens, and some simple pictures.

Preparation: This outlines anything you need to do or prepare before starting the activity. Most of the activities are low in preparation, so this might involve dividing the board into columns or cutting up some paper.

Time guide: This provides a general guide as to how long the activity could take. Many of the activities have flexible timing and they can be shortened or extended to fit the time you have.

Activity: This gives a description of the activity divided into stages, and provides examples of teacher-talk that you could use with the children.

Variations: This shows you how you could use the same activity with small alterations to vary the activity or to revise different vocabulary or grammar. It also shows ways of extending the activities to get even more from them.

Conclusion

I hope you and your children enjoy the activities in this book. I also hope that you will take the ideas and make them your own, adapting and adding to them to suit your children and circumstances. I wish you and your learners lots of fun and positive experiences with English.

Activities

1 Disappearing cats

LANGUAGE   Vocabulary you wish to revise (about 8–12 items)

RESOURCES   The board, a picture, or flashcard for each vocabulary item

PREPARATION   Divide the board into two sections with a vertical line and draw a simple cat in each section of the board.

TIME GUIDE   5–10 minutes

Activity

1   Tell the children that one of the cats is theirs, and the other is yours – you could let them choose which cat is theirs. The children could also name the cats.

2   Show them the pictures or flashcards and quickly check the vocabulary that you want to revise. For example:

What's this? Is this a lion?

3   Shuffle the flashcards, and then select one without letting the children see what it is.

4   Ask the children to try and guess which picture you have chosen. They can ask questions:

Is it an elephant?

5   For each wrong guess, rub out one part of their cat – an ear, the tail, a leg, the whiskers, and so on. When they guess correctly, rub out a part of your cat. Continue by selecting another flashcard.

6   This activity works well if you make rubbing out the parts of the cat something of a drama. For example:

Oh, no! Your cat hasn't got any ears!

Finally, see whose cat disappears first – yours or the children's!

2 Changing places

LANGUAGE	Revision of vocabulary used for describing people; colours, clothes, parts of the body, adjectives
RESOURCES	One chair for each child
PREPARATION	Create some space to arrange the chairs in a large circle in the middle of the classroom.
TIME GUIDE	5–10 minutes

Activity

1 Get all the children to sit on the chairs arranged in a circle.

2 Pre-teach the phrase *change places* by asking pairs of children to change places a couple of times.

3 Stand in the middle of the circle and call out an instruction based on what the children are wearing or look like. For example:
Change places if you are wearing jeans.
Change places if you have got blue eyes.
Change places if you are six years old.
Change places if you are wearing something green.

4 The children who fit the instruction, must all stand up and change places by moving to another chair. When they stand up to change places for the first time, quickly remove one chair so that there is one chair too few.

5 The one child who did not get a chair to sit on now comes into the centre of the circle. With your help (if necessary) he or she calls out another instruction.

6 As the children fitting the instruction change places, the child in the centre should also try to sit down. Again, whoever is left without a chair comes into the middle and calls out the next instruction.

7 To add an extra element of fun, you can add the instruction *All change*. When you say this, all the children have to change places.

3 Crossing the river

LANGUAGE   Vocabulary or letters of the alphabet you wish to revise (about 12–14 items)

RESOURCES   A picture or flashcard to represent each vocabulary item or selected letter of the alphabet

PREPARATION   Create some space across the middle of the classroom.

TIME GUIDE   10 minutes

Activity

1   Use the cleared space in the classroom and place the flashcards in a line on the floor with the pictures facing up.

2   Divide the class into two teams, with one team standing at each end of the line of pictures.

Rock, paper, scissors

3   If necessary check that the children know how to play 'Rock, paper, scissors' by practising this with the whole class.

rock   paper   scissors

Each child stands opposite another child with their fists clenched. They both move their fists up and down as they count *1*, *2*, *3* together and out loud. On the third count each child chooses between showing rock, paper, or scissors with their hand.

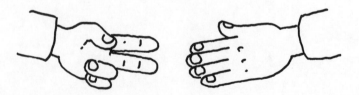

One child wins; rock beats scissors, paper beats rock, and scissors beats paper. If the same gesture is chosen by both children, they simply repeat the game until one of them wins.

4 The first child from each team walks along beside the line of pictures, each starting at opposite ends of the line. They have to take turns to say what each picture or letter is as they reach it. The rest of their team can join in by saying each item.

5 When the two players meet they play 'rock, paper, scissors'. Whoever wins stays where they are, and the other player goes to the back of their team's line.

6 The next player in the losing team now starts walking along the line of pictures saying what each picture is, and the winning player also continues. When they meet, they play 'rock, paper, scissors'.

7 This continues until one team member manages to cross the river, in other words, reaches the opposite end of the line of pictures. A point is scored for each child that crosses the river.

8 The game can end when all of one team reach the other side – but that could take a very long time! Or you can play for a set period of time, stopping when you choose, and the winning team is the one with the most points or with the player furthest along the line.

Variation

Rather than using items of vocabulary to be revised, use a selection of letters from the alphabet that your learners are having difficulty with.

4 Board races

LANGUAGE	Vocabulary you wish to revise (about 8–12 items), and in Variation 2 the question form of grammatical structures you wish to revise: *Do you like…? Can you…? Have you got…?*
RESOURCES	A picture or flashcard of each vocabulary item
PREPARATION	None
TIME GUIDE	10 minutes

Activity

1   Place the pictures on the board and check that the children know the vocabulary: *What's this? Is this a pizza?*

2   Divide the class into teams so that you have three to four teams. Draw an imaginary line on the floor about a metre from the board and line the teams up behind the line.

3   Say one of the items displayed on the board. The first child from each team races to touch the correct picture.

4   You can also revise grammatical structures by saying the vocabulary item in a short simple sentence. For example, *I like cheese.*

5 A point is given to the team that touches the right picture first. The runners then go to the back of their line and the next child in each team has a turn.

....

Variations

1 Tell the children that you are thinking of one of the pictures on the board, and they should guess which one. One child from each team takes turns asking you questions: *Is it cheese? Is it chocolate?* Once someone has guessed the right word, the first child from each team races to touch the correct picture.

2 Choose a structure to practise with the vocabulary items in the pictures: for example, 'like' for food vocabulary, 'can' for sports activities, or 'have got' for classroom objects. Each team takes turns to ask a question to guess what picture you are thinking of. For example:

Do you like cheese?

Can you swim?

Have you got a pencil case?

Respond to the children's questions. For example:

TEACHER   *I like one of these things. What do I like?*

CHILD A   *Do you like cheese?*
TEACHER   *No, I don't.*

CHILD B   *Do you like ice cream?*
TEACHER   *No, I don't.*

CHILD C   *Do you like fish?*
TEACHER   *Yes, I do!*

Once they have guessed the correct picture, the first child from each team races to touch the correct picture.

5 Three chairs

LANGUAGE   Revision of prepositions of time *in*, *on*, and *at*. In the Variation, any vocabulary set that you wish to revise.

RESOURCES   Three chairs

PREPARATION   Place three chairs in front of the board, and create some space around them.

TIME GUIDE   5–10 minutes

Activity

1   Label the chairs in front of the board, by writing on the board above each one. Label them: *in*, *on*, and *at*.

2   Divide the class into two or three teams, and ask them to line up about one metre in front of the chairs.

3   Say a time expression that requires one of the prepositions *in*, *on*, or *at*. For example: *the morning, 6 o'clock, Tuesday, Christmas, June.*

4   The first child in each team races forward to sit on the appropriate chair for that phrase. For example, if you say *June*, the children race to be first to sit on the chair labelled *in*.

5   The first child to sit on the correct chair earns one point for their team. The next child from each team then has a turn, and this continues.

Variation

The activity can be done with different vocabulary from three different categories instead of prepositions. For example, the chairs can be labelled *food, animals,* and *clothes*. With older children you can focus on parts of speech, labelling the chairs, *noun, verb,* and *adjective*. Alternatively, again for older children, label the chairs *past, present,* and *future* and rather than reading out words, read out whole sentences.

6 Circular questions

LANGUAGE	Food vocabulary and *Do you like …?* with affirmative and negative short answers. In the Variation, a range of verb patterns that you wish to revise.
RESOURCES	Pictures or flashcards of about 10 food items
PREPARATION	Prepare enough space for the children to be able to stand or sit in a circle.
TIME GUIDE	5–10 minutes

Activity

1 Get the children to sit on their chairs or stand in a circle in the space you have created. You should also be part of the circle.

2 Take one of the pictures, turn to the child on your right, and ask a question, for example, *Do you like apples?* The child answers: *Yes, I do,* or *No, I don't.*

3 The child then takes the card, turns to the person on their right and asks the same question. This continues round the circle, so that they all ask and answer the question.

4 Once the questioning is underway, start off another question, using another vocabulary item, in the opposite direction. Then add more questions in both directions so that there are several questions going round the circle at the same time. The questions can all have the same structure, for example, they can all be *Do you like …?* questions, or they can vary. (See below for suggestions.)

5 The fun really starts once there are several questions going round the circle at the same time. There will be quite a lot of noise and chaos!

6 The questions should all go right round the circle, with the pictures being returned to the teacher once the circle has been completed.

Variation

Other grammatical structures and vocabulary sets can be used. For example, use activities or musical instruments to revise *Can you …? Yes, I can. / No, I can't.* or *Do you like + -ing …?*; use places to revise *Did you go to … yesterday? Yes, I did. / No, I didn't.*; use objects to revise *Have you got a …? Yes, I have. / No, I haven't.*

7 Do as I say, not as I do

LANGUAGE	Parts of the body, actions *jump*, *touch*, *turn*
RESOURCES	None
PREPARATION	Create some space in the middle of the classroom.
TIME GUIDE	5–10 minutes

Activity

1 Get all children to stand up – ideally in a space in the middle or at the front of the classroom, away from their desks and chairs.

2 Give a series of simple instructions with actions for the children to copy. For example:

Jump.

Clap your hands.

Touch your ear.

Touch your knees.

Close your eyes.

3 Tell the children to: *Do as I say, not as I do*. Give an instruction, but when giving the instruction you should do a different action. For example, say *Touch your toes* while you touch your ear.

4 The children need to listen to the instruction and follow what you say, rather than simply watch your actions and follow what you do.

5 After a couple of practice turns, those that make a mistake and follow what you do rather than what you say are 'out'. Those children can then act as monitors, or alternatively you could ask them to give the instructions. The last child not to be called out is the winner.

8 Spot the differences

<table>
<tr><td>LANGUAGE</td><td>Vocabulary and grammatical structures you wish to revise – the language will depend on the chosen story.</td></tr>
<tr><td>RESOURCES</td><td>A few pictures to represent the key aspects of a short story or a storybook from a previous lesson.</td></tr>
<tr><td>PREPARATION</td><td>None</td></tr>
<tr><td>TIME GUIDE</td><td>10 minutes</td></tr>
</table>

Activity

1 Remind the children of a story that you have told the class before. Use a story book or pictures from the story and ask questions to elicit key facts and events. For example:

Can you remember the story we read last week?

Who was in the story?

What happened to…?

2 Explain that you are going to re-tell the story, but you're having a bit of a bad day and seem to be making lots of mistakes. Ask them to listen carefully for anything that is 'wrong' in your version of the text.

3 When they hear a difference between your version of the text and the original, they should wave their arms in the air and shout out the correction. For example:

TEACHER   *Today it's Jack's birthday. He's eight years old.*
CHILDREN   *No! He's not eight, he's nine!*
TEACHER   *Oh, yes, I remember now – sorry! OK, he's nine years old, but he's not having a party.*
CHILDREN   *No! He is having a party!*

4 If the story comes from a course book or from a graded reader, the children can be following it as you read the text. This would combine reading and listening.

9 Beat the teacher

LANGUAGE	Vocabulary you wish to revise
RESOURCES	The board
PREPARATION	None
TIME GUIDE	5–10 minutes

Activity

1 Tell the children that you are going to play a game called 'Beat the Teacher!' Write *Teacher* and *Class* in the corner of the board to keep the score.

2 Tell the children that you are going to start drawing one of the words from today's lesson. Explain that you are going to draw it bit by bit and that they have to try and guess what it is. Tell them they will have three chances to score points. Begin by drawing just one line or curve of the item.

3 Ask the children if they know what it is. If they can identify it from just one line, they get three points.

4 If they can't guess it, draw another bit of the picture and let them have another guess.

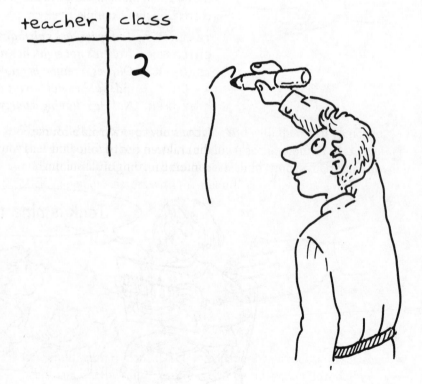

5 If they guess it correctly this time, they get two points.

6 If they still haven't guessed, draw another bit of the picture. If they guess it correctly this time, they get one point.

7 Draw another part of the picture. If the children still can't guess what it is, you get three points. If they do guess it correctly, they stop you getting any points, but they don't get any points either.

8 Finish drawing the picture. Or ask one of the children to come up and finish the drawing.

....

Variation

If you are not good at drawing, or if the words are difficult to represent visually, you can do the same activity with letters. You need to leave spaces for the missing letters to give some indication of the length of the word. You could put in dashes for the missing letters to make the activity easier. For example, if one of the words you want to revise is *excited*, the board could look like this:

Step 1: __ __ __ __ *t* __ __ (three points for the class)

Step 2: __ __ __ __ *t* __ *d* (two points for the class)

Step 3: *e* __ __ __ *t* __ *d* (one point for the class)

Step 4: *e* __ __ *i* *t* __ *d* (three points for the teacher)

10 Circle time

LANGUAGE	Revision of personal information questions (spoken)
RESOURCES	None
PREPARATION	Create a space for the children to sit or stand in a circle.
TIME GUIDE	5 minutes

Activity

1 At the start or end of the lesson ask all the children to come and sit or stand in a circle in the space you have created.

If this is the first time you are doing the activity, choose a question that the children are very familiar with, for example; *What's your name?* or *How are you today?*

2 Drill the question a couple of times with the whole group. Then get them to ask you the questions, so that you provide a model of how to answer. For example:

CHILDREN   *What's your name?*
TEACHER   *My name's Marta.*
CHILDREN   *How are you?*
TEACHER   *I'm fine thank you.*

3 Once you're sure the children are comfortable with the question, turn to the child on either your left or right and ask them the question. He or she answers and then turns to the person next to them and asks them the same question. This continues all the way round the circle until the question comes back to you.

4 As they learn more questions during their lessons, you can begin using them. Here are some examples:

What's your favourite colour?   *What sports do you like?*

What's your favourite food?   *How old are you?*

Variations

1 You can 'send' a question in either direction round the circle at the same time.

2 Once you have done this activity a few times and the children have at least three to four questions that they are confident with, let them choose which question they want to ask.

3 Rather than go round in a circle, make a name card for each child. (If possible, they can write their own name cards and decorate them.) Place the name cards face down in the middle of the circle. Choose one card, and ask that child a question. This child then chooses a name card and asks that person a question. This continues until all name cards have been used.

11 Spelling races

LANGUAGE	Vocabulary you wish to revise the spelling of (eight or more items)
RESOURCES	The board
PREPARATION	Divide the board into columns, with one column per team.
TIME GUIDE	5–10 minutes

Activity

1 Divide the class into teams of about six to eight children.

2 Line each team up in front of one of the columns already drawn on the board.

3 Give the first person in each team a piece of chalk or board pen.

4 Say a word that you want to revise or test the spelling of.

5 The first person from each team steps up to the board and writes the first letter of the word. They then pass the chalk or board pen to the next person in the team who has to write the next letter. This continues until one team has the full word written on the board. The players are allowed to help each other in their team by telling each other what letter comes next.

6 The moment one team has finished (even if not correct) say *Stop!* All the teams must stop writing.

7 Encourage the other teams to tell you if the completed word is correct or not. If the word is spelt correctly, the team gets a point.

8 The game continues with a new word each time.

Variations

1 An extra rule can be added: if someone makes a mistake, the next player can correct it, but they can't then add the next letter. For example, if the word is *apple*, and one team has *apl* on the board, the next person in the team can change *l* for *p* – but they can't now write *l* as well.

2 Rather than say the word you want them to spell, which can provide clues as to how it's spelt, show a picture of the vocabulary item. Alternatively, you could say a synonym or antonym. For example, if you say *cheap*, the children write *expensive*.

12 Personal questions

LANGUAGE	Revision of personal information questions (written)
	What's your favourite colour?
	What time do you get up?
	How do you get to school?
	Have you got any brothers or sisters?
RESOURCES	Small squares of paper
PREPARATION	Cut some paper into small squares to make about 20 pieces for a group of three children.
TIME GUIDE	15 minutes initially, then 5–10 minutes

Activity 1

1 You need to create a list of about twelve questions asking for personal information. Choose one of the following ways to do this.

Divide the class into pairs or small groups and ask them to write down as many questions asking for personal information as they can think of. Monitor the groups as they are writing in order to help with any mistakes.

If you are working with a course book, encourage the children to look back through their course books and notebooks to find suitable questions.

Brainstorm possible questions with the class and write them up on the board. You can either elicit the questions from the children, or ask them to come up and write on the board themselves.

Activity 2

1 Choose one question to demonstrate with, and show the children how to write down each word of the question on one square of paper. Explain that they shouldn't use capital letters, that they should add a question mark to the last word of the question, and that contractions, *who's*, *what's*, should be regarded as one word. Each question should be written in the same handwriting.

2 Divide the class into pairs or groups of three and ask each pair or group to choose two to four questions from the list prepared in Activity 1.

3 Give each pair or group about 20 small squares of paper. Ask them to write their chosen questions on the paper squares – one word per square, as demonstrated.

4 Ask the children to mix the pieces of paper together and then pass them on to another pair or group. Make it clear that they shouldn't look at the squares of paper until you say *Go!*

5 When you say *Go!* the pairs or groups then race to put the words in the correct order to re-make the questions.

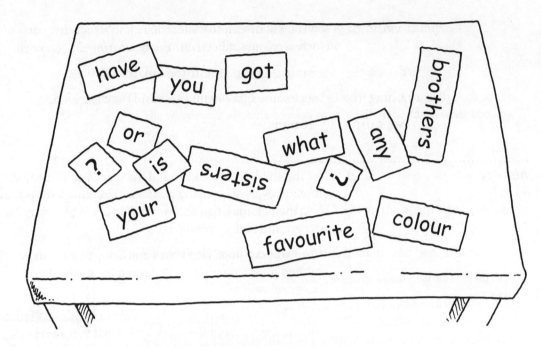

6   Once the questions are made, they can ask and answer the questions in their pairs or groups.

7   This can then be repeated, with the children mixing up the questions again and passing them on to another pair or group.

Variations

1   Prepare the jumbled questions before the class if you want to work with specific questions only, or if the question writing stage would be too difficult for the children.

2   At the start of the next lesson, hand out the sets of jumbled questions (randomly) and ask the children to repeat the activity.

3   Make bigger sets of jumbled questions, by combining the questions from two or three pairs or groups (so that you have six to eight questions in a set). Divide the class into larger groups and ask them to work together to re-construct all the questions.

4   Time the children while they are re-constructing the questions at the start of the next lesson. Then time them again to see if they can make the questions faster than the previous time. Once a group has made their questions, they should go and help another group. This keeps the task cooperative, with everyone working together.

5   A final extension task, which works well with smaller classes, is to mix all the jumbled questions together. Time the children as they re-make the questions. Repeat the activity in the following lesson – can they do it faster?

13 Fact or fiction?

LANGUAGE	Revision of descriptive vocabulary and structures; parts of the body, clothes, colours, adjectives, *You're wearing …*, *You've got …*
RESOURCES	Some background music (optional)
PREPARATION	Create some space in the middle of the classroom.
TIME GUIDE	5–10 minutes

Activity

1 Ask the children to walk around the space you've created, looking closely at everyone, paying particular attention to how they look; their clothes, hair colour etc. You could play music in the background at this point.

2 When you say *Stop!*, clap your hands, or pause the music, the children must stop walking and stand back to back with whoever they are closest to.

3 They take it in turns to make true statements about their partner from memory: about how they look, what they're wearing, the colour or length of their hair, the colour of their eyes and so on. For example:

You're wearing a blue T-shirt.

You've got brown eyes.

4 Each time an incorrect statement is made, their partner scores a point. For example,

CHILD A *You've got brown eyes.*
CHILD B *Yes, you're right!*

CHILD B *You're wearing a blue T-shirt.*
CHILD A *No! Sorry, you're wrong! One point for me!*

This continues until you say *Go!*, clap your hands, or start the music again.

5 Each time you ask them to stop, they must find a new partner to stand back to back with. The idea is to try and make more correct statements than your partner each time.

28

14 Find the similarities

LANGUAGE	Descriptive vocabulary: colours, shapes, objects, actions (depending on the pictures used); *there is / there are*, the present continuous
RESOURCES	A class set of a course book, enough for one per child
PREPARATION	Select two different pictures from the course book: the pictures don't need to be connected or related, but ideally there will be some similarities between them.
TIME GUIDE	5–10 minutes

Activity

1 Give the children a course book and divide the class into pairs. Ask them to decide who is Child A and who is Child B. Tell Child A to look at one of the pictures you have selected, and Child B to look at the other picture. They must not show each other their pictures.

2 Working in their pairs, they try to find similarities between their pictures. They can do this by asking questions, for example, *Is there a car in your picture?* or by making statements about their picture, for example, *There is a car in my picture.*

3 Encourage them to consider things like objects, actions, colours, materials, shapes, and patterns.

4 After a period of time, 2–5 minutes, ask them to stop and find out how many similarities they found. Ask different pairs to tell you some of the things they found. To close the activity, let them look at each other's pictures and see if they can find any more similarities.

Variations

1 If you think the children might find it difficult to get started, get all those working with the same picture to talk together for a few minutes to brainstorm vocabulary, sentences, and ideas about their picture before working with their partners to find the similarities.

2 If you are not working with a course book, you can use pictures from magazines or newspapers.

15 Disappearing dialogues

LANGUAGE	Vocabulary and structures you wish to revise; the dialogue you choose will dictate the language revised.
RESOURCES	A short dialogue (no longer than about 30 words) from earlier in the lesson or from a previous lesson
PREPARATION	Write the short dialogue on the board, in fairly large and clear letters.
TIME GUIDE	5–10 minutes

Activity

1 Ask the children to read the dialogue written on the board in chorus. You could divide the class into A and B parts, with each group only saying their relevant lines.

2 Now, rub out or cover a couple of the words and repeat the process, chorusing the dialogue, including the missing words.

> A   What would you like to eat?
>
> B   I'd like pizza and salad, please.
>
> A   Would you like a drink?
>
> B   Yes please, I'd like an orange juice.

> A   What would you like to   ?
>
> B   I'd like   and   , please.
>
> A   you like a drink?
>
> B   Yes   , I'd like an orange juice.

3 Continue by rubbing out or covering more and more of the dialogue each time. The challenge for the children is to be able to remember all the parts of the dialogue that have disappeared.

16 Guess which picture

LANGUAGE	*Yes / No* questions using a variety of structures including *Is it …?*, *Is there …?*, *Are there …?*, the present continuous
RESOURCES	A class set of a course book with a number of pictures in it, enough for one between two or three children
PREPARATION	None
TIME GUIDE	5–10 minutes

Activity

1 Divide the class into groups of two or three and give each group a course book. If you are using a course book with your class, ask them to take out their books and sit in groups.

2 Open your book at an interesting picture but do not show it to the class.

3 Tell the class they must find out which picture you are looking at. Tell them they can look in their own course book and ask you *Yes / No* questions. They should not ask questions like, *Is the picture in unit 7?* but rather questions like, *Is the picture outside?*

4 To make sure everyone participates, you could elicit one question from each group to begin with.

5 After a few minutes of questions, the children should be able to identify the picture. If they need help, you can provide a clue, for example:

It's in unit 7.

It's in units 1–3.

It's in the first half of the book.

6 Repeat the activity as many times as there is interest!

Extension

Play the game a few times until the children are familiar with the rules and the types of questions they can ask. Write a few example questions on the board for the children to refer to during the following stage. Now, ask them to play the game without you, working in pairs or groups. One child chooses a picture and the rest of the group ask questions to find the correct picture.

17 Pass the pen

LANGUAGE   Vocabulary or grammar you wish to revise (See *Variations* below
               for suggestions.)

RESOURCES   Strips of paper, background music (optional)

PREPARATION   Cut some sheets of A4 paper up into strips and prepare pictures or
               flashcards of vocabulary items (optional).

TIME GUIDE   5–10 minutes

Activity

1   Divide the class into small groups of four. Ideally they should sit
    round a table or a flat surface.

2   Give each group a small pile of paper strips (ten or twelve strips
    depending on the number of items you want to revise) and a
    board pen.

3   Explain that while the music is playing (or the teacher is singing),
    they should pass the pen around the group.

4 When the music stops, the child holding the pen is the writer, and he or she is the only one who can touch the pen. The rest of the team can help and offer contributions, but they can't touch the pen.

5 The teacher gives a word to write down by showing a picture, defining an item, miming a word, or saying the opposite word and the child holding the pen writes the word on a strip of paper. For example, if you are revising adjectives, when the music stops you can say: *What's the opposite of clean?* The child holding the pen writes *dirty* taking help or advice from others in their team if necessary.

6 The first team to finish writing the word hold up their strip of paper and say *Stop!*

7 The other teams look to check if the word is spelt correctly, and if so a point is awarded to that team and the game continues, with the music starting again and the pen being passed around.

....

Variation

This game can also be used to revise various grammar points. For example:

Comparatives and superlatives – say an adjective and the teams have to write the comparative form (and the superlative form if also being revised).

Irregular verbs – say the infinitive form of a verb and the teams have to write the past form (and past participle form if also being revised).

18 First letter–last letter race

LANGUAGE	Learner-generated vocabulary
RESOURCES	The board
PREPARATION	Divide the board into columns so that there is one column per team.
TIME GUIDE	5–10 minutes

Activity

1 Divide the class into teams of about six to eight children and ask them to line up in front of the board.

2 In each column, near the top, write the same 'start word'. This is the word that starts the chain of words that each team is now going to create; for example, *snake*. It really doesn't matter what the word is, as long as each time you play the game you choose a word that ends in a different letter, as if the 'start word' always ends in '*e*' the children can recreate the same chain of words each time.

3 Give the first person in each team a board pen or a piece of chalk. When you say *Go!* the first person from each team writes a word under the 'start word'; it must begin with the same letter that the start word ends with. The first player then gives the board pen or chalk to the next person in their team who has to write a word beginning with the same letter as the last letter of the previous word. For example:

snak**e** – **e**g**g** – **g**reat

4 The players continue taking turns to create a word chain linking the first and last letters, and the game continues for a set period of time.

5 When you say *Stop!* all the teams must stop writing. Ask the teams to check each other's word chains to ensure that all the words follow on correctly.

6 You can use the following ideas to decide which team has 'won' the race:

You only get points for words that the other team(s) don't have in their word chains.

You only get a point if the word is spelt correctly.

Words have to be connected to a particular theme or topic, for example, animals or food, that you announce at the start of the game.

Words have to have more (or fewer) letters than the word above.

Rather than having a time limit, teams have to race to write a chain with a certain number of words, for example, ten or twelve.

19 Sentence noughts and crosses

LANGUAGE	Vocabulary or grammar you wish to revise; for example, prepositions of place, the verb to *be*
RESOURCES	The board
PREPARATION	Make a noughts and crosses grid (3 x 3)* with a word in each square. The words you allocate to each square will depend on what you wish to revise.
TIME GUIDE	10–15 minutes

Activity

1 Draw a noughts and crosses grid (3 x 3) on the board and number each square.

2 Divide the class into two teams; one noughts and one crosses.

3 Ask the noughts team to choose a square: *Square number 3, please.*

4 Read out the word that you allocated to that square on your prepared grid. The team then have 30 seconds to decide on a sentence using that word. The sentence needs to be meaningful and true. For example, if you wanted to revise prepositions of place, in each square there could be a preposition such as *in*, *on*, *under*, *behind*. If the team get the word *under*, they could create a sentence such as: *Our school bags are under our desks.*

5 Once their time is up, the team say their sentence out loud and the other team (along with the teacher) decide if it is an acceptable sentence or not. If it is acceptable, the team wins that square on the board and the teacher marks it with a nought. If the sentence is not correct, the square remains 'free'.

6 The game continues with the crosses team now choosing a square.

7 The first team to get three noughts or three crosses in a row wins the game.

* Noughts and crosses is a grid game, played against an opponent. The idea of the game is to get either three noughts or three crosses in a row – horizontally, vertically, or diagonally – while stopping your opponent from doing the same.

20 Picture test – true or false?

LANGUAGE Vocabulary and grammatical structures you wish to revise – the language will depend on the pictures used.

RESOURCES A class set of a course book which has a number of pictures

PREPARATION Select a busy picture from the course book and prepare some *true / false* statements about the picture.

TIME GUIDE 10–20 minutes

Activity 1

1 Distribute the course book so that the children have one book each, or one between two.

2 Ask all the children to turn to the picture you have selected, and allow them one minute to look at the picture and to try and remember as much as they can about it.

3 While they are looking at the picture, think of some true and false statements about it. (You could prepare the statements in advance.)

4 Ask them to close the books after one minute. Test the children's memory with true and false statements about the picture. For example:

There are three people. True or false?

The boy is eating an ice-cream. True or false?

Activity 2

1 Divide the class into groups of about four. If you have enough course books you can divide them into pairs.

2 Ask each group or pair to look through their course book and choose a picture to make their own true and false statements about.

3 Ask them to write a number of statements about the picture they have chosen. It is important to remind them to make some true and some false. If you only have a short time available, they could simply think of statements rather than write them down.

4 Go around the room and label each group A or B. Ask a group A and a group B to work together.

5 Group A asks group B to look at the picture they chose in the course book for one minute. The book is then closed and group A test group B's memory with their prepared true and false statements.

6 This is then repeated with group B testing group A on their picture.

21 Create a story

LANGUAGE   Learner-generated vocabulary and grammar

RESOURCES   The board

PREPARATION   None

TIME GUIDE   10–20 minutes

....

Activity

1 Draw a small picture on the board. It can be of anything and should be simple, taking no more than about 20 seconds to complete.

2 Select 10–12 children and ask them to stand in a line in front of the board. Allow them about 20 seconds to draw their own small picture on the board. There should be no talking at this stage in the activity so that the children don't tell each other what to draw.

3 Once they have completed their pictures, quickly circle each one to separate it from the others near it. Ask the children to return to their seats.

4   Explain that they are now going to use these pictures to create a story. Start the story off by making a sentence using one of the pictures. Label this picture number 1.

5   Ask the children to contribute the next sentence of the story, making use of another of the pictures on the board as a prompt for the sentence. Once a sentence has been provided, write number 2 next to that picture. The aim is to use the picture prompts to create a story so it's important that the second sentence links to the first sentence.

6   Continue eliciting sentences, and numbering the pictures. When all the pictures have been used, the story is 'finished'.

7   It might be necessary to recap the story every now and then. Encourage the children to tell you as much as they can remember as you point to each picture. You can guide and prompt if necessary to help with the English or to keep the story on track.

Variations

1   Alternatively, divide the class into groups after step three. Continue to build the story as a class, with each group taking it in turns to think of the next sentence to contribute to the story.

2   If you are not doing this activity for the first time, or if you are working with a particularly strong group, after step 3 above divide the class into groups of three or four and ask them to create their own stories. The stories can be spoken, or written if you have enough time.

3   If they have worked in groups to create their own stories, ask two groups to work together. Group A tells group B their story, and group B tries to identify the order of the pictures as they listen, making a note of the order on a piece of paper. Group B then does the same for group A.

22 Twenty questions

LANGUAGE   Learner-generated *Yes / No* questions

RESOURCES   The board

PREPARATION   Divide the board into three columns.

TIME GUIDE   5–10 minutes

Activity

1   Elicit and write a list of famous people in the first column on the board. As the children call out names, make sure that the others know who the person is. You can write the names up, or the children can come up and write one person each.

2   Tell the class that you are one of the famous people listed on the board and that they need to work out who you are by asking you *Yes / No* questions; that means your answer can only be *Yes* or *No*. So they can ask, for example; *Are you a man?* but not *Are you a man or a woman?* You can limit the number of questions they are allowed to ask before making a guess – usually the limit is twenty questions.

3   As they ask the questions, write them in the second column of the board. This is so that the children can refer to them later. Some suitable questions are as follows:

Are you a man?

Are you on TV?

Are you in a band?

Are you in films?

Are you a singer / an actor / a sportsperson?

Have you got blue eyes / brown hair / short hair?

Are you young?

4   In the third column, to guide the children in their questioning, make a note of each 'fact' they establish. For example:

Are you a man? Yes: write **man** on the board.

Are you in films? No. Are you in a band? Yes: write **band** on the board.

5   Once you have done this as a class, the activity can be done in pairs or small groups. You could briefly brainstorm some more example *Yes / No* questions and write them in the second column to help the children further with possible questions.

6   Each child then secretly chooses one of the names on board and writes it on a piece of paper. Their partner, or the others in their group, then asks *Yes / No* questions to guess who they are.

23 Letter dictation

LANGUAGE	Letters of the alphabet
RESOURCES	None
PREPARATION	Select a sentence from the lesson or one that uses the language covered in the lesson.
TIME GUIDE	5–10 minutes

Activity

1 The sentence you select for this activity should be one that uses language that has recently been taught in class or that has occurred in their course book. For example, if a previous lesson was focusing on the present continuous the sentence could be: *She is riding her bike.* Or if the language was food vocabulary: *He has cereal and toast for breakfast.*

2 Ask the children to get a pen and a piece of paper. Explain that you will read out some letters and they should write them down.

3 Dictate the letters from the sentence you have chosen to work with, but don't group the letters to form the words as you would normally. Add breaks in random places. For example:

S [pause] H E I [pause] S R I [pause] D I [pause] N G H E [pause] R B [pause] I [pause] K E

4 The children now work in pairs or on their own to try and work out what the sentence should be.

5 The children can then choose or write their own sentences to dictate to the rest of the class in the same way.

24 Ladders

LANGUAGE   Vocabulary you wish to revise

RESOURCES   The board

PREPARATION   Divide the board into two or three columns depending on the number of teams. Draw a ladder with 8–10 steps in each column.

TIME GUIDE   5–10 minutes

Activity

1   Divide the class into two or three teams (depending on the number of children) and ask each team to line up in front of the board. Explain to them that you are going to ask the teams to write one word connected to a topic on each step of their ladder.

2   Choose a topic area that you have studied with the class recently, such as daily routines, school, food, free time. Write the topic at the top of the board and say *Go!*

3   The first person in each team writes the first word on the bottom step of the ladder. They then pass the pen to the next person and they write the next word and so on.

4   Once one team has a word on each step of the ladder, everyone stops writing. You can ask them to put their hands on their head, or sit down and fold their arms to indicate that they have finished.

5   Points are awarded for each word that is connected to the topic. The team that finished first also earns a bonus point. The following 'extra' rules for points can be introduced:

Only those words that are spelt correctly earn points.

Only those words which don't appear on any of the other ladders earn points.

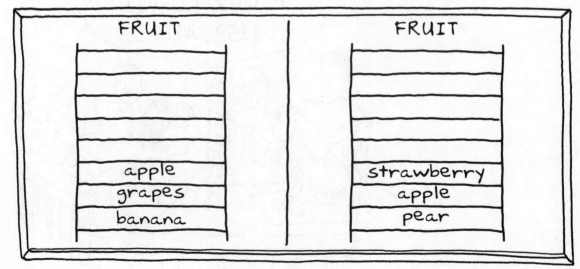

25 Whisper chain

Variations

1 Each team is given a slightly different topic. For example, if you are doing furniture, one team can be given the kitchen, another the bedroom, and so on.

2 The teams have to write words that are the same number of letters or more as they go up the ladder.

25 Whisper chain

LANGUAGE	Vocabulary and grammar you wish to revise
RESOURCES	The board
PREPARATION	Think of a short list of things in English your class can draw.
TIME GUIDE	5–10 minutes

Activity

1 Divide the class into teams of about six to eight children. If possible make the teams even.

2 Divide the board into as many columns as you have teams. Ask the children to line up in their teams in front of one of the columns on the board. If there is space, encourage them to stand a little apart from each other, maybe an arm's length away from the child in front of them. (If this is not possible, the activity will still work.)

3 Give the person at the front of each team a piece of chalk or a board pen.

4 Stand yourself at the back of the team lines and ask the last person in each team to come closer to you.

5 Whisper a noun or a short instruction that can be drawn relatively quickly and easily on the board. For example:

apple

chair

T-shirt

cat

Draw a fat cat.

Draw a big square.

The idea is that the word or instruction will be whispered from child to child and the first person from each team will have to draw the item on the board.

6 Once all of the teams have the word or instruction, say **Go!** Each child whispers the word or instruction to the next person in their team.

7 When the child at the front of the team 'receives' the word, they draw it on the board.

8 Two points are awarded to the team that have the right item drawn on the board and that finished first. If other teams have the right item, they get one point. Any teams that have drawn the wrong thing don't get any points.

9 Repeat with new words or instructions. Make sure that there is a new person in front of the board, and that the previous person goes to the back of the team line. The board can be wiped clean after each round, or the instructions can build on each other. For example:

Draw a fish in the square.

Draw a circle next to the square.

26 Words from a word

LANGUAGE	Learner-generated vocabulary
RESOURCES	The board
PREPARATION	None
TIME GUIDE	5 minutes

Activity

1 Choose a reasonably long word, like; *elephant, television, computer, chocolate, helicopter, sandwich*. Alternatively, use a short phrase or combination of words, such as; *apple pie and custard, I like apples, Happy Christmas*. Write the word or phrase on the board.

2 Explain that the task is to make as many words as possible using only the letters from the word written on the board within a set time.

3 Demonstrate what you mean by showing them one or two possible words and one or two words that are not possible. For example, using the word *elephant: Look, from ELEPHANT, we can make 'hat' – H, A, T (pointing to the letter) and we can make 'pen' – P, E, N. But we can't make 'pear' – look, P, E, A, but there's no R; and we can't make 'apple' – look – A, P, but there's only one P. Can you tell me some other words we can make from ELEPHANT?*

4 Now, ask the children to work in pairs or small groups of three or four. Each pair or group needs a pen and a piece of paper.

5 Write a new word or short phrase on the board and set a short time limit of about one or two minutes. The children work in their pairs or groups to make as many words as possible from the word on the board.

elephant

hat ant pen
neat ten hen

6 Once the time period is up, ask one pair or group to start reading out their list of words. The other pairs or groups (and the teacher) should listen carefully for any words that are not possible. For each word that is possible, the other pairs or groups should tick them off if they have the same word on their lists.

7 Once the first pair or group have finished reading out their words, the other pairs or groups should read out any other words they have on their lists that have not already been read out.

8 The pair or group with the most words that no other group found is the winner!